The River Fiddlers

Printed in Canada
Designed by Jon Dennis
First Printing, 2017
ISBN 9780994958310

Herman's Monster House Publishing
Fredericton, N.B.
www.monsterhousepublishing.com

Dedication

Lucy, family, friends and for anyone, big or
small who loves adventures, loves music and
loves building memories

The Old Canoe Maker busied himself around his shop, cleaning and wiping his tools. He stroked his long beard as he worked.

The Old Canoe Maker was very excited because he had heard that a Fiddle Man was coming to the nearby village to play his fiddle. The village was a long way down the river, but the Old Canoe Maker was determined to go.

The Fiddle Man was famous because of the happy musical sounds he could make playing his fiddle. People would dance, sing and clap their hands when they heard his music.

The Old Canoe Maker loved fiddles as he had heard them being played when he was a child a number of years ago and he very much wanted to hear that music again.

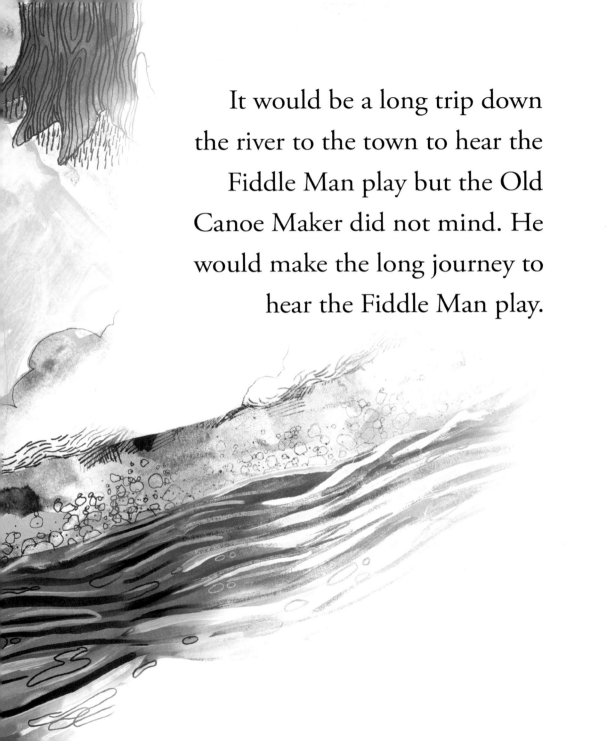

It would be a long trip down the river to the town to hear the Fiddle Man play but the Old Canoe Maker did not mind. He would make the long journey to hear the Fiddle Man play.

The Fiddle Man played wonderful music. He played Irish jigs and Scottish reels and lovely, dreamy waltzes. One couldn't help but dance when he played his magical tunes.

The Old Canoe Maker enjoyed
every second of the Fiddle Man's
music, and when the crowd had
left the Old Canoe Maker stayed
behind to meet the Fiddle Man
and thank him.

What work do you do?" The Fiddle
Man asked the Old Canoe Maker.

"I make canoes for people
to paddle on the river"
the Old Canoe
Maker replied."

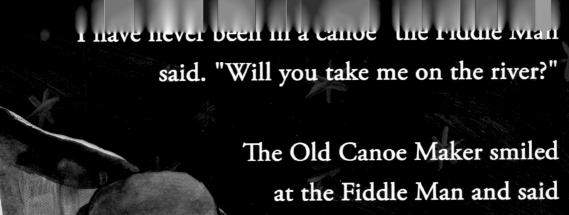

"I have never been in a canoe" the Fiddle Man said. "Will you take me on the river?"

The Old Canoe Maker smiled at the Fiddle Man and said "I will take you on the river if you play your fiddle for me as we go."

The next day dawned bright and
sunny as the Old Canoe Maker
and the Fiddle Man set out.

The river was quiet and flowing
gently, and the sun shone warmly
as they drifted downstream. The
Old Canoe Maker paddled his
canoe and the Fiddle Man
played his fiddle.

The Old Canoe Maker and the
Fiddle Man became best friends
and enjoyed their trips down the
river each summer.

People from near and far heard of
the Old Canoe Maker's and the
Fiddle Man's happy trip on the river
and they wanted to join in.

The next summer people brought canoes, fiddles, and other instruments to the river. The fiddle players played their fiddles and all the people sang as they coasted and paddled down the river in their canoes.

Each summer more and more people came. The Old Canoe Maker and the Fiddle Man were pleased that they could make so many people happy with this simple pastime of listening to music on a gentle and happy river.

The sound of magical music coming
from many canoes on the river
became an annual event and many
people came from all different parts
of the world to watch and listen.

A little History

In June, 2003 Ron was interested in writing an article for a magazine on the "Fiddles on the Tobique." Valerie and Ron met with Helen Edgar and Bill Miller and learned about the history of the fiddlers on the tobique.

Ron and Valerie didn't have their own canoe so they watched from the banks of the Tobique as 759 canoes and 100 musicians floated down the river playing their instruments. Tunes like "Big John McNeil" and "Amazing Grace" took on a new tone being played on a slow-moving river.

Ron was quite taken with the whole event and later contacted Bill with the idea of a children's story. Sadly Ron became ill and passed away in October, 2004 before he and Bill were able to do much more than pass drafts of the story back and forth.

In 2016 Bill and Valerie were finally able to complete Ron's dream by publishing "The River Fiddlers."

The Old Canoe Maker

William "Bill" Victor Miller III was born on August 17, 1945. He spent 59 years living on the Tobique River. He is still building wooden canoes, carrying on a three generation family business for 45 years. In 2012 he was awarded the Queen Elizabeth Diamond Jubilee Medal for the contribution the Fiddles on the Tobique has made for the Arts and Culture of New Brunswick and Canada. It was his idea to put a fiddle player in a wooden canoe and sail down the Tobique river to Riley Brook. The idea caught on quickly and the tradition of making music on the beautiful Tobique continues. Mr. Kirk Whipper, founder of the Great Canadian Canoe Museum in Peterborough, Ontario, once said on one of his many visits to the event, "Fiddles on the Tobique is a Canadian National Treasure" Bill is also a salt water sailor, storyteller and a nature photographer.

The Artist Bennie Allain

Bennie Allain was raised in PEI in the late 80s and early 90s. His whimsical artwork has graced the covers of many Canadian folk and rock albums. He has published his own designs of playing cards as well as Tarot-style cards and is prolific when it comes to drawings based on puns. He is currently spending his time in a camper near the Yukon River in Dawson City.